Solid Foundation Sermon Starters

LIFE OF DAVID

*Blueprints for 30 messages
built upon God's Word*

Steve Jones

Cincinnati, Ohio

Dedicated to my wife, Tami, and my children, Stephen and Katie

All Scripture quotations, unless otherwise indicated, are taken from the HOLY BIBLE, NEW INTERNATIONAL VERSION®. NIV®. Copyright © 1973, 1978, 1984 by International Bible Society. Used by permission of Zondervan Publishing House. All rights reserved.

Cover design by Grannan Graphic Design LTD

Interior design by Robert E. Korth

Edited by Jim Eichenberger
© 1999 by Standard Publishing
All rights reserved.
Printed in the U.S.A.

Solid Foundation is an imprint from
Standard Publishing, Cincinnati, Ohio.
A division of Standex International Corporation.
06 05 04 03 02 01 00 99   5 4 3 2 1

Contents

Picking a Winner	1 Samuel 16:1-13	5
God's Tool Chest	1 Samuel 16:14-23	7
Victorious Faith—Part 1	1 Samuel 17:12-44	9
Victorious Faith—Part 2	1 Samuel 17:34-52	11
The Jealousy Cycle	1 Samuel 18	13
God's Protection	1 Samuel 19	15
Keys to Great Friendship	1 Samuel 20	17
David's X-Files	1 Samuel 21, 22	19
Prepare to Meet Your *Dune*	1 Samuel 23, 24	21
God's Restraining Order	1 Samuel 25	23
Sleeping With the Enemy	1 Samuel 27, 29. 30	25
The Lord's Anointed	2 Samuel 1:1–2:7	27
Changing of the Guard	2 Samuel 35	29
Handle With Care	2 Samuel 6; 2 Chronicles 13–15	31
When God Says "No"	2 Samuel 7	33
The Heart of God	2 Samuel 9, 21	35
Try a Little Kindness	2 Samuel 10	37
Prepped for Disaster	2 Samuel 11:1-4	39
The Tangled Web—Part 1	2 Samuel 11:4-15	41
The Tangled Web—Part 2	2 Samuel 11:16-27	43
Reality Check	2 Samuel 12:1-7	45
Rebound—Part 1	2 Samuel 12:7-13	47
Rebound—Part 2	2 Samuel 12:14-31	49
Paean to Forgiveness	Psalm 32	51
Reconciliation	2 Samuel 13, 14	53
When the Bottom Falls Out	2 Samuel 15	55
Turn the Other Cheek	2 Samuel 16:5-14; 19:18-23	57
Keys to Motivation	2 Samuel 18:1–19:8	59
Passing the Baton	1 Kings 1, 2	61
Write Your Own Eulogy	2 Samuel 23:1-7	63

Picking a Winner
1 Samuel 16:1-13

The account of Samuel's anointing of David illustrates how God can help us "pick a winner" when it comes to the various people we will partner with in life. Making a right choice in this regard is of serious consequence. Furthermore, the world's "buzz" on making such a choice cannot be trusted. Samuel's example in recognizing God's choice is helpful to us.

I. THE NEED FOR PICKING A WINNER (v. 1)

A. Samuel needed to pick a winner because whoever he picked would be the next king of Israel. Being the king was an important job requiring great character and leadership. Likewise we need to make good choices when selecting people to fill important roles in our lives and churches, i.e., mates, elders, teachers, political leaders, or business partners.

B. Samuel also needed to pick a winner for the spiritual welfare of the nation. Saul's sin (see 1 Samuel 15) had already resulted in grief for Samuel. A new leader, devoted to God, would result in healing and joy. Whether or not we experience peaceful and happy circumstances in life often depends upon our aptitude for picking "winners."

II. THE "BUZZ" ON PICKING A WINNER (vv. 2-7)

A. The "buzz," or conventional wisdom, for picking a winner is to focus on superficialities. When Samuel laid eyes on tall, good-looking Eliab, he assumed that this was the right man for the job. But God said that he wasn't. God told Samuel that men have an unfortunate tendency to make judgments based on "outward appearance."

B. We must be careful not to fall victim to conventional wisdom when it's our turn to choose. There is nothing wrong with physical attractiveness per se (David was handsome), but when it really matters, a hard body and a pretty smile are no substitute for character.

III. THE KEY TO PICKING A WINNER (vv. 7-13)

A. Pray to God. Samuel conversed with the Lord in the process of choosing the next king. God gave him insight, allowing him to make a choice beyond the limits of the common wisdom. God will give us insight when we pray (James 1:5).

B. Listen to words. Jesus said, "Out of the overflow of the heart the mouth speaks" (Matthew 12:34). The words of David's pastoral Psalms were already revealing the content of his heart.

C. Watch for deeds. Jesus said, "By their fruit you will recognize them" (Matthew 7:20). David demonstrated his servant's heart by shepherding sheep. As we observe people's actions we can discern whether they are good trees or bad trees.

ILLUSTRATIONS

Appearances can be deceiving. A man visited the opera and while sitting in the very back row, fell in love with the voice of the lead soprano. After a whirlwind courtship they were married. On the wedding night the groom watched in anticipation as she prepared for bed. She took off her wig and placed it on a stand, pulled out her false teeth and put them in a jar of water, plucked out her glass eye and laid it in a dish, and unstrapped her artificial leg and leaned it on the wall. In horror the groom stared at her and cried, "For goodness sakes, woman, sing, sing, sing!"

Choosing God's way. A tourist driving down a deserted road came face to face with a sign that said: "Road closed. Do not enter." As the road ahead looked pretty good, he ignored the sign and drove on. A few miles later he came to a bridge that was down. He promptly turned around and retraced his route. As he reached the point where the warning sign stood, he read the words on the other side: "Welcome back, stupid!"

(If we've tried the conventional wisdom for picking a winner, we know it doesn't work. Now let's try God's way.)

God's Toolbox
1 Samuel 16:14-23

How does God work in this world? Does he have a certain plan and pattern that he follows with slavish consistency? This passage demonstrates for us the variety of tools that God has in his "toolbox" to carry out his sovereign will.

I. THE EVIL SPIRIT (v. 14)

A. The inspired author says that an "evil spirit from the Lord tormented Saul." How can an evil spirit come from the Lord? The answer lies in the truth of God's sovereignty. He is ultimately in control and can use even Satan and his emissaries as a means to discipline his people.

B. This is no different from God using a godless nation like Assyria as "the rod of my anger" to discipline his people (Isaiah 10:5, 6). Consider also the fact that Satan had to seek permission from God, and was restricted by God, before tempting Job (Job 1, 2).

C. Knowing the sovereignty of God in this area gives Christians great assurance, for it protects us from being ravaged by the evil one. Paul assures us that God will not allow Satan to tempt us beyond our ability to endure (1 Corinthians 10:13).

II. WISE COUNSELORS (vv. 15-22)

A. It was more than coincidence that Saul's attendants advised him to seek out a musician to provide relief for his torment. And it was more than coincidence that David himself had caught the attendants' eyes. This was the providence of God who used these counselors to open the door for David's training in the royal court. The counselors were tools of God.

B. The qualities that these attendants valued revealed the wisdom of their counsel. They recommended David because they knew him to be a man of courage, action, good speech, good looks, and musical talent (v. 18). If we listen to counselors who love what God loves, he can use them to bless us!

III. MUSIC (v. 23)

A. Music is a tool of God. It is interesting to note that whenever the evil spirit came upon Saul, David would play his harp and the evil spirit would depart. God's Word reveals the prominence of music in the spiritual realm. When Elisha was about to inquire of God, he said, "'Now bring me a harpist.' While the harpist was playing, the hand of the Lord came upon Elisha" (2 Kings 3:15). During the reign of David, over 4000 musicians were assigned to sing in the temple night and day (1 Chronicles 9:33; 23:5).

   B. It is the mark of Spirit-filled Christians to sing and make melody in their hearts to the Lord and speak to each other in psalms, hymns, and spiritual songs (Ephesians 5:18-20).

CONCLUSION

All created things are tools of God for his glory and purposes. As the Sovereign, he can use any variety of means to accomplish his goals. The three tools we have discussed are only the beginning. What we must remember, is that we too can be instruments of his will. When we willingly cooperate with that will, we are used and blessed in the process.

ILLUSTRATIONS

It could be worse! Because of a minor infraction, a sailor aboard the USS Reeves, bound for Japan, was busted one rank, fined and given extra duty for three weeks. Looking forward to celebrating his twenty-first birthday on July 2, he consoled himself every night during his extra duty by reciting, "They can bust me, they can fine me—but they can't take away my birthday." As July 2 approached his excitement increased. When he went to bed on July 1, he happily repeated, "They can bust me, they can fine me—but they can't take away my birthday." The next morning, he found out that the ship had crossed the international date line—and it was July 3.

(As bad as this world is, if it weren't for God's sovereign control over the malevolence of Satan, things would be hopelessly worse.)

Wise counsel from unexpected sources. A fox, a wolf, and a bear went hunting and each got a deer. A discussion followed about how to divide the spoils. The bear asked the wolf how he thought it should be done. The wolf said everyone should get one deer. Suddenly the bear ate the wolf. Then the bear asked how the fox proposed to divvy things up. The fox offered the bear his deer and then said the bear ought to take the wolf's deer as well. "Where did you get such wisdom?" asked the bear. "From the wolf," replied the fox.

Victorious Faith—Part 1
1 Samuel 17:12-44

William Arthur Ward said, "Adversity causes some men to break, others to break records." Which category we fall into is determined by our faith. By facing and defeating Goliath, David demonstrated the characteristics of victorious faith.

I. VICTORIOUS FAITH BEGINS HUMBLY (vv. 12-24).

A. David was faithful in the small things—obeying Dad, watching the sheep, and carrying supplies. David was doing what he was supposed to do while the army of Israel was not. That's a big reason why David rose to the top.

B. Often, in this day of mediocrity, all it takes to stand out in the crowd is faithfulness in whatever God has given us to do today. Performance evaluations take place every day—not every six months or every year.

II. VICTORIOUS FAITH SEES THE POTENTIAL REWARD (vv. 25, 26).

A. Whoever killed Goliath was going to receive a lot of money, marry into the royal family, and be tax-exempt for life. When David heard that he did a double-take! Contemplating the reward, David was encouraged. Yet material gain was obviously not the only reward he considered. He knew that even greater rewards awaited those with a zeal for Jehovah. His courage overcame his fear.

B. Instead of focusing on all of the possible negative fallout of facing up to our giant, we must focus on the rewards. We already have negative fallout from *living* with the giant. The giant is not going away. While facing him is risky, God offers a spiritual and emotional jackpot when we trust in him.

III. VICTORIOUS FAITH DOESN'T LISTEN TO CRITICS (vv. 28-44).

A. David had to deal with at least three critics.
1. Eliab criticized David's motives: "I know how conceited you are and how wicked your heart is" (v. 28).
2. Saul criticized David's lack of experience: "You are not able to go out against this Philistine and fight him; you are only a boy, and he has been a fighting man from his youth" (v. 33).

  3. Goliath criticized David's ability: He "saw that he was only a boy . . . and he despised him" (v. 42).

 B. Critics create "solution pollution." When striving for victories in personal growth, work, family, or church, don't cater to the critics. They won't like it, but we can do it anyway because God gives us permission.

IV. VICTORIOUS FAITH IS CONFIDENT (v. 32).
 A. The army of Israel was overwhelmed by Goliath's aggression, reputation, and intimidating appearance. He was beating up the army of Israel without even fighting. In their minds they had already resigned themselves to slavery.

 B. David won the psychological battle because of his confidence. He had confidence in God and himself. Both kinds of confidence are necessary. God-confidence without self-confidence paralyzes. God doesn't move until we step out in faith. Self-confidence without God-confidence exposes us. To depend on our own strength and not the Lord's is to be vulnerable to the attacks of the enemy. Greater is he that is in me than he that is in the world.

ILLUSTRATIONS

A great fight. It was an outstanding case in a small Western mining town. Joe was brought in on an assault charge. The state presented the weapons he used: a huge telegraph pole, a dagger, a pair of shears, a saw, a gun, and a Civil War saber. Counsel for the defense produced the weapons used by the alleged victim to defend himself: a scythe, a hoe, an ax, a shovel, and a pair of tongs. After deliberating, the 12 men of the jury filed in slowly and the foreman read the verdict: "We the jury would give $500 to have seen that fight!" (That's the way I feel about the story of David and Goliath!)

Confidence. There is a story about an oilman from Texas who went to Heaven. Nice as it was, the Texan kept bragging about how in his state everything was even better. At last Saint Peter got weary and took the oilman to the edge of Heaven so that he could look straight down into hell. "Have you got anything like *that* in Texas?" The Texan said, "No, but I know some good ol' boys in Houston who can put it out for you."

While this confidence is unsubstantiated vanity, David's confidence was based in faith in the God of Israel!

Victorious Faith—Part 2

1 Samuel 17:34-52

Booker T. Washington said, "You can't judge success by the position you have but by the obstacles you had to overcome to get there." People who reach giant positions in life have defeated giants. As David demonstrates, such obstacles are only overcome by victorious faith. Note four more characteristics.

I. VICTORIOUS FAITH BUILDS ON PAST EXPERIENCE WITH GOD (vv. 34-37).

A. The hand of God had protected and delivered David in the past, and he drew on that experience to lift him up to face a higher level of challenge.

B. Nothing builds our faith like the actual experience of realizing victory through the power of God working in us. As we face our giants today we should remember God's faithfulness to us in the past.

II. VICTORIOUS FAITH ACTS NATURALLY (vv. 38-40).

A. David refused Saul's armor, not because it was too big, but "because he was not used to them" (v. 39). Trusting the Lord, David stayed in character and went into battle clothed with the full armor of God (Ephesians 6:11-18).

B. During a crisis, people will try to make us like them. Saul wanted David to wear his armor, but all the armor in Saul's armory wasn't going to help David win this victory. God only expects us to use what *we* have to overcome our giants.

III. VICTORIOUS FAITH KNOWS A HIGHER PURPOSE (vv. 45-47).

A. When David went to face his giant, he wanted more than a personal victory and more than the reward. He wanted to glorify the living God of Israel. When Jesus talked to his disciples after his resurrection he gave them the Great Commission—a purpose for their lives—to spread a message that would glorify God.

B. We may accomplish many victories and successes in our lives; but if we can't direct those to the glory of God, they will become twisted and perverted. Success without a godly purpose, results in despair.

IV. VICTORIOUS FAITH ELEVATES OTHERS TO A HIGHER LEVEL (vv. 48-52).

A. The men of Israel arose and shouted and charged the enemy when they saw what David had done. These were the same ones who had previously been cowering in their tents for forty days.

B. One reason it's important for us to take on the giant and win by God's grace is because we don't live in a vacuum. Our successes and failures affect those around us. Dishonorable conduct drags others down. Honorable conduct lifts them up.

ILLUSTRATION

The importance of a higher purpose. All he ever wanted in life was more. He wanted more money, so he parlayed inherited wealth into a billion dollar pile of assets. He wanted more fame, so he broke into the Hollywood scene and soon became a filmmaker and star. He wanted more sensual pleasure, so he paid handsome sums to indulge his every sexual urge. He wanted more thrills, so he designed, built, and piloted the fastest aircraft in the world. He wanted more power, so he secretly dealt political favors so skillfully that two U.S. Presidents became his pawns. All he ever wanted was more. He was absolutely convinced that more would bring him true satisfaction. Unfortunately, history shows otherwise. This same man, who literally had it all, ended his life the exact opposite of how he lived most of it—emaciated, colorless, sunken chest, grotesque fingernails, rotting black teeth, tumors, and innumerable needle marks from his drug addiction. He died a billionaire junkie, insane by all reasonable standards. His name . . . Howard Hughes.

The Jealousy Cycle
1 Samuel 18

Every sin has a life cycle beginning with temptation and ending in death (James 1:14, 15). Saul's relationship to David graphically illustrates the cycle of one sin in particular —jealousy.

I. THE SEEDS OF JEALOUSY (vv. 1-9)

A. The seeds of jealousy were sown in Saul's heart by unfavorable comparisons between himself and David (vv. 7, 8). The Bible warns us of the folly of comparing ourselves to others (Galatians 6:4).

B. The seeds of jealousy were sown in Saul's heart by his own insecurity. He worried that David would steal his kingdom (v. 8). The Christian's security is in the Lord and his provision (1 Corinthians 4:7).

II. THE FRUIT OF JEALOUSY (vv. 10-27)

A. Violence is a fruit of jealousy. Saul hurled his spear at an unsuspecting David in an attempt to "pin David to the wall" (v. 11). When jealousy takes root in the heart the fruit of violence is not far behind.

B. Fear is a fruit of jealousy. Three times in this chapter the inspired author says that Saul was afraid of David (vv. 12, 15, 29). Of course, the fear was irrational and unjustified. David was completely loyal to Saul. But sin clouds the mind and darkens the heart (Romans 1:21).

C. Intrigue is a fruit of jealousy. Three times Saul plotted and schemed to "have David fall by the hands of the Philistines" (v. 25). Each of these cabals was counterproductive with David becoming more successful than before. The sin of jealousy will cause one to squander precious time and resources in futile intrigues rather than "making the most of every opportunity" (Ephesians 5:16).

III. THE PITS OF JEALOUSY (vv. 28, 29)

A. Broken fellowship with God is a pit in the fruit of jealousy. Saul realized that the Lord had left him and was with David (vv. 12, 28). This continuing broken fellowship with God was due, in part, to Saul's jealousy of, and hateful treatment toward David. The Bible says that no one can love God and hate his brother at the same time (1 John 4:20).

B. Broken fellowship with men is a pit in the fruit of jealousy. Saul was David's enemy until the day he died (v. 29). What a sad observation. Saul's blind jealousy caused him to trash a valuable friendship. Truly, those who bite into the fruit of jealousy wind up choking on the pit.

CONCLUSION

The destructiveness of Saul's jealousy cycle makes clear why Paul lists the sin of jealousy with other acts of the sinful nature that prevent people from inheriting the kingdom of God (Galatians 5:20, 21).

ILLUSTRATIONS

The futility of comparisons. An MG Midget pulled alongside a Rolls-Royce at a traffic light. "Do you have a car phone?" its driver asked the guy in the Rolls. "Of course I do," replied the Rolls driver. "Well, do you have a fax machine?" The driver in the Rolls sighed. "I have that too." "Then do you have a double bed in the back?" the Midget driver wanted to know.

Quickly, the Rolls driver sped off. That afternoon he had a mechanic install a double bed in his auto. A week later, the Rolls driver passes the same MG Midget, which is parked on the side of the road—back windows fogged up and steam pouring out. The arrogant driver pulls over, gets out of the Rolls and bangs on the Midget's back window until the driver sticks his head out. "I want you to know that I had a double bed installed," brags the Rolls driver.

The Midget driver is unimpressed. "You got me out of the shower to tell me that?"

No enemies. A reporter was interviewing a centenarian on his hundredth birthday. The elderly man declared "I'm 100 years old today and I don't have an enemy in the world." Impressed, the reporter said, "How inspiring! How did you manage that?" The old man retorted, "Outlived every one of them."

(Whether we end our lives with peace among friends, or in strife among enemies, depends more on *how* we have lived than on how *long*.)

God's Protection

1 Samuel 19

As David fled from Saul he must have felt vulnerable. The most powerful man in the country wanted him dead! What is more, he may have had nagging doubts about the justice of his persecution. After all, hadn't David been assured that he had found God's favor while Saul had rejected the very One who empowered him to serve?

Yet this experience had a purpose. By studying it we can observe some of the ways in which God protects his children.

I. FOND FRIENDS (vv. 1-7)

A. Jonathan's friendship with David became a source of God's protection. Jonathan spoke to his father on David's behalf and brought about a temporary reconciliation. On more than one occasion Jonathan warned David of Saul's malevolent intentions.

B. "There is a friend who sticks closer than a brother," counsels Solomon (Proverbs 18:24). Sometimes God uses the friends in our lives to deliver a word of warning, encouragement, or challenge for our own protection.

II. FAST FEINTS (vv. 8-10)

A. As David sat innocently playing his harp Saul flung a spear at him trying to pin him to the wall. David's actions may seem obvious and natural, but they are also quite instructive. David *eluded* Saul and fled. He dodged, and then he got *out* of Dodge.

B. At times we are protected through our own God-given instincts to *run*. "Flee the evil desires of youth" (2 Timothy 2:22). What do you do when your boss, spouse, preacher, or any person in authority over you begins to unjustly heave spears in your direction? Don't pick them up and throw them back. Instead, become skilled at dodging out of the way.

III. FAITHFUL FAMILY (vv. 11-17)

A. Saul sent soldiers on a covert mission to kill David as he slept in his own house. David's wife Michal warned him and facilitated his escape through a window.

B. Paul said that love "always protects" (1 Corinthians 13:7). This is true in the Christian family. Husbands, wives, parents, and children can form the living walls of protection in a godly refuge for one another.

IV FRUSTRATED FOES (vv. 18-24)
  A. Three times Saul sent his soldiers to Naioth to capture David. Each time they wound up being frustrated by the direct intervention of God's Spirit. David's would-be captors became prophets! Indeed this is what happened to Saul when he went himself.

  B. God usually works his protection in a subtle, seemingly indirect fashion. But on rare occasions he directly intervenes to frustrate the foes of his children.

CONCLUSION
During adverse times in our lives, we may feel as if we're under assault by enemies. David was assaulted by the might of Saul, however he was protected by the even greater power of Jehovah. When we reflect upon times of crisis, we too may realize that God has still been protecting us in a variety of wonderful ways.

ILLUSTRATIONS
The need for a protector. The new platoon commander addressed his men for the very first time. "Who in this unit thinks he can whip me in a fight?" After several moments of silence one large, burly soldier stepped forward, looked the commander in the eye, and responded "I do sir." "Very well," said the commander, "you are now my sergeant, my second in command." Addressing the platoon again he said, "Now who thinks he can whip my sergeant in a fight?"

The wisdom of dodging. A soldier went to his chaplain for counsel over his fear of being killed in battle. The chaplain said, "Son, there's no sense in fretting over it. If the bullet has your name on it, you're going to go and there's nothing you can do about it. If the bullet doesn't have your name on it, then you're safe." The soldier replied, "That may be true, but the bullet I'm worried about is the one inscribed 'To whom it may concern'!"

Keys to Great Friendship

1 Samuel 20

Everyone wants good friends. We are told that the key to having friends is being a friend. While true, that may be more easily said than done. How does one go about being a friend?

One of the great friendships of history was David's relationship with Jonathan. By studying their alliance we discover six keys of a great friendship.

I. TRANSPARENCY (vv. 1-3)

A. David was completely honest with his friend Jonathan concerning his troubles, even though Jonathan's father was the cause. Jonathan was just as forthright about his conviction that David's fear was unfounded.

B. The strongest bonds are created by those who allow their friends into the most secret places of the heart, revealing their greatest hopes, dreams, and sometimes, fears.

II. CONCERN (vv. 4-9)

A. Jonathan and David had a genuine concern for one another's welfare. Jonathan said, "Whatever you want me to do, I'll do it for you."

B. Everyone needs a friend who cares enough to do whatever it takes to help them in time of need.

III. COMMITMENT (vv. 14-17)

A. Jonathan and David made a covenant with each other, swearing fidelity for all time. Indeed, they stayed friends through thick and thin until parted by death.

B. Fair-weather friends are common. We must cultivate the ties that bind our hearts in Christian love.

IV. LOYALTY (vv. 30-34)

A. Jonathan defended David's integrity to his own father, Saul, and at risk to his own life.

B. A test of great friendship is what we say of our friends when they're *not* present and are attacked by people of influence. Fierce loyalty builds lasting friendship.

V. PASSION (v. 41)

A. When David and Jonathan realized they might never see each other again, they kissed each other and wept together. David wept even more than Jonathan.

B. Great friendships are characterized by strong feelings. We (especially men) must not be embarrassed to express our emotions.

VI. GOD (v. 42)

A. David and Jonathan's friendship had a spiritual dimension to it: "We have sworn friendship with each other in the name of the Lord."

B. To reach the highest level, friendships must be based upon more than common interests and affinities. Great friendships are built upon a mutual faith and commitment to the Lord.

CONCLUSION

"A friend loves at all times, and a brother is born for adversity" (Proverbs 17:17). Like David, in the most difficult trials of our lives we may discover the secrets of a great and godly friendship.

ILLUSTRATIONS

The need for true friendship. Two men were camping out in the wilderness when they were awakened in the early morning by the sound of a roar. They peeked out of their tent to see a huge grizzly bear racing down the hillside right for them. One of the men ducked back in the tent and calmly began putting on his running shoes. His friend said, "Are you crazy? Do you think that you can outrun a grizzly bear?" To which the first man replied, "I don't have to outrun the bear; I just have to outrun *you*."

Loyalty. Bill McCartney, former coach and now founder of Promise Keepers, tells of a loyalty ritual at the beginning of each season. He would have each of his players come forward, two by two, to the front of the locker room, stand back to back and pledge that from that moment on they would always speak words of loyalty and support for one another whether speaking in their presence or behind their back!

David's X-Files
1 Samuel 21, 22

Lily Tomlin once said, "One of the chief causes of stress in today's world is reality." At various times in life we all face circumstances of extreme difficulty that call for us to stretch our faith and obedience. David's experience shows the extent we must be willing to go to extremes with God in order to be victorious over our enemy.

I. EXTREME HUNGER (21:1-6)
A. David, continuing his flight from the mad pursuit of Saul, approached an isolated priest named Ahimelech for bread. The only bread available was some bread consecrated unto God. Being extremely hungry, David ate the consecrated bread.

B. Jesus condoned this action in Matthew 12. When our appetite for righteousness is as extreme as David's appetite for bread, we will feast on God's Word and renew our strength. "'Rabbi, eat something.' . . . 'My food,' said Jesus, 'is to do the will of him who sent me and to finish his work'" (John 4:31, 34).

II. EXTREME WEAPON (21:8, 9)
A. David, being unarmed, was vulnerable, so he asked the priest if a weapon was available. Ahimelech answered that the sword of Goliath was stored behind the ephod. David took the weapon saying, "There is none like it." It was an extremely effective weapon.

B. A Christian is engaged in a battle like no other, an extreme struggle against "the powers of this dark world and against the spiritual forces of evil" (Ephesians 6:12). Therefore we must have an extreme weapon, and we do—"the sword of the Spirit, which is the word of God" (Ephesians 6:17). Paul said, "The weapons we fight with are not the weapons of the world. . . . they have divine power to demolish strongholds" (2 Corinthians 10:4).

III. EXTREME CREATIVITY (21:10-15)
A. While in the jurisdiction of King Achish, David exercised extreme creativity to protect himself. He feigned insanity by drooling and acting crazy. Achish was fooled and David continued unharmed.

B. In our zeal for the lost we Christians are to exercise extreme creativity in our methods of evangelism. "I have become all things to all men so that by all possible means I might save some" (1 Corinthians 9:22). If necessary, we will be fools for Christ.

IV. EXTREME COMPANY (22:1, 2)

A. There gathered around David a most unusual company of men described as "all those who were in distress or in debt or discontented." David became their leader and they fought loyally together for life.

B. No Christian is called to solitary discipleship. Our journey of faith is fortified by a most peculiar company of pilgrims, all united by an extreme commitment to Christ and one another. "Come to me, all you who are weary and burdened, and I will give you rest" (Matthew 11:28).

V. EXTREME BURDEN (22:6-23)

A. David felt that a careless oversight of his had resulted in the unjust death of a faithful priest at the hands of wicked King Saul. David had an extreme burden for the welfare of others.

B. Likewise, Christians carry an extreme burden for those who are lost and have no hope outside of Jesus Christ. "Woe to me if I do not preach the gospel!" (1 Corinthians 9:16).

CONCLUSION

Halfhearted commitment to God is inadequate on the road of discipleship. God calls for an extreme commitment—all of our heart, mind, soul, and strength.

ILLUSTRATION

Extreme company under extreme duress—After a grueling day of training, which had included a ten-mile hike and completion of a difficult obstacle course, a platoon of raw recruits quickly fell into bed. As one of the platoon, a Christian, lay in the dark, he recited a prayer aloud: "Now I lay me down to sleep, I pray the Lord my soul to keep; if I should die before I wake, *thank you, Jesus!*"

There was a brief pause and then several voices said in unison, "Amen."

Prepare to Meet Your *Dune*

1 Samuel 23, 24

Nothing seems as desolate as a desert. The image of miles of shifting, lifeless landscape, a land of sand dunes and the unfiltered rays of sun, speaks of despair and hopelessness.

Yet the experience of David illustrates that even in the desert our God is with us. In these two chapters David's flight from Saul takes him through three different deserts. In each one he deepens his knowledge of God in a distinct way.

I. THE DESERT OF ZIPH—GOD'S STRENGTH (23:14-16)

A. "Day after day Saul searched" for David. How exhausting and discouraging this must have been for the young man who knew in his heart he had done nothing to deserve such treatment. In the midst of this desert David was helped by Jonathan to "find strength in God."

B. We have entered our "Desert of Ziph" when all seems lost in hopeless despair. However, we too can "find strength in God," for Paul describes God as the "Father of compassion and the God of all comfort, who comforts us in all our troubles" (2 Corinthians 1:3, 4). God's strength sustains.

II. THE DESERT OF MAON—GOD'S SUSPENSE (23:24-28)

A. In this desert, Saul began closing in on David. David and his men had managed to stay just out of Saul's reach, but they were slowly losing ground. At the very last minute "a messenger came to Saul, saying, 'Come quickly!'" Philistines were attacking back home. So Saul broke off his pursuit of David and went to meet the Philistines. David and his men must have sat down, breathed a collective sigh of relief, and looked up toward Heaven as if to say "It's about time!"

B. The desert of Maon is where we learn that while God can be trusted to step in and rescue his children, he sometimes waits long enough for them to feel the hot breath of disaster on their necks before he does. Why? Because it's the only way to purge us of that self-reliant, independent spirit that hinders our faith in God from fully developing. He is the "God, who tests our hearts" (I Thessalonians 2:4).

III. THE DESERT OF EN GEDI—GOD'S SOVEREIGNTY (24:1-22)

A. In the desert of En Gedi, while pursuing David to take his life, Saul unwittingly placed himself in an incredibly vulnerable position. David had the opportunity to kill Saul, but instead David entrusts himself to the sovereignty of God saying: "May the Lord be our judge and decide between us. May he consider my cause and uphold it; may he vindicate me by delivering me from your hand" (24:15).

B. The desert of En Gedi represents a time when we are tempted to exact revenge on those who have unjustly caused us pain. We may even find ourselves with a perfect opportunity to do so. But Jesus taught us to leave the business of vengeance in the hands of God: "When they hurled their insults at him, he did not retaliate; when he suffered, he made no threats. Instead, he entrusted himself to him who judges justly" (1 Peter 2:23). God is sovereign. He's in control. Leave it to him.

CONCLUSION

Moses, Paul, Jesus, and David all had their times of testing in the desert where they came to know God in a fresh way. Prepare to meet *your* dune.

ILLUSTRATION

Trusting God's sovereignty. In 1980, America entertained the world at the Olympics in Lake Placid. I remember coming home from church the Sunday that America was playing Russia in hockey. It was in the end of the first period, and we were beating the Russians. All of a sudden I realized my stomach was in a knot. My knuckles were white, and I had this anxiety about the game. All through the second period we were ahead. Going into the third period, I knew what would happen. The Russians would score five goals at the end of the game, beat us, and we would be embarrassed again. But we won!

It was such a big deal that the national networks played it again. I watched the whole thing Sunday night. Only this time I didn't have a knot in my stomach. I leaned back on the couch and put my feet up. What made the difference? I could relax because I knew the outcome.

When we have faith that God is working for our eternal good, we can have amazing peace even when we *don't* know the outcome.

God's Restraining Order
1 Samuel 25

Christians look forward to the "sweet by and by," the glory of Heaven, where we can enjoy all of God's gifts with abandon. Unfortunately, however, we live in the "nasty now and now." In this world our battle with our fallen nature is still in progress. We must learn to allow the Spirit to restrain our sinful impulses. David's dealings with Nabal remind us of the virtues of restraint.

I. THE OBSTACLES TO RESTRAINT (vv. 1-22)

A. Injustice (vv. 3, 10, 11)—David experienced injustice at the hands of Nabal who withheld from David the compensation due him for his protection. This injury to David was not imagined or exaggerated.

B. Pride (vv. 12, 13)—David's pride was offended as he was insulted by Nabal in the presence of his fighting men. It's tempting to retaliate when you feel your reputation is at stake.

C. Power (v. 13)—David had four hundred fighting men armed with swords at his disposal. People in power have a tendency to take action against others simply because they can. "Might makes right." But does it?

D. Emotion (vv. 20, 21)—David ranted aloud to his men as he rode toward vengeance. He was full of passionate anger and was getting more and more irate as he went. Most impulsive actions are taken in the heat of the moment.

II. THE REASONS FOR RESTRAINT (vv. 23-31)

A. Sinful Nature (v. 25)—Abigail asked David to exercise restraint because Nabal was a wicked fool. Sin has a tendency to muddle people's thoughts (Romans 1:21) so that they don't act justly or sometimes even rationally. Abigail suggests that foolishness be taken as a mitigating factor.

B. Innocent Bystanders (v. 25)—Abigail informs David that if *she* had been present when his men arrived events would have transpired differently. Abigail was righteous and likely would have been harmed in David's planned attack. Innocent bystanders get hurt in the cycle of revenge.

C. God's Promise (vv. 28-30)—Abigail reminded David of the many promises that God had made to him including establishing him as king, keeping him alive, and punishing his enemies. An effort at restraint would represent an exercise in faith by David.

   D. Potential Regrets (v. 31)—Abigail suggests that, unless David restrains himself, a day would come when he would "have on his conscience the staggering burden of needless bloodshed." The pain of restraint weighs ounces, regret weighs tons.

III. THE BLESSINGS OF RESTRAINT (vv. 35-42)
   A. Unexpected Resources (v. 35)—David exercised restraint and God blessed him with unexpected resources from the hand of Abigail. When we trust God instead of taking matters into our own hands, God is able to make up for material loss. See Luke 18: 29, 30.

   B. Renewed Faith (v. 39)—When wicked Nabal died of "natural" causes David praised God and credited him for upholding his cause. Restraint leaves room for God to act and faith to grow.

   C. Clear Conscience (v. 39)—David said God "has kept [me] from doing wrong." With the clarity of 20/20 hindsight, David understood that if he had acted on his rash impulses he would now be guilty of wrongdoing.

   D. Positive Relationships (vv. 39-42)—The widow Abigail becomes David's wife. They are able to begin their relationship on a solid foundation because of David's restraint. How unlike David's later marriage to Bathsheba which, because of his lack of restraint, was marred by a cloud of suspicion, guilt, and corruption.

CONCLUSION
There's only one thing worse than being wrong, and that's staying wrong when you know you're wrong. When God gives a restraining order, take heed and obey.

ILLUSTRATION
The wisdom of restraint. At a military social function the commanding general of the base delivered a welcoming oration. A young second lieutenant muttered to the woman at his side, "What a pompous old windbag he is." The woman replied, "Lieutenant, do you know who I am?" "No ma'am." "I am the wife of that old windbag, as you call him." "Indeed," said the lieutenant, "and do you know who *I* am?" "No, I don't," said the general's wife. "Thank goodness," said the lieutenant, as he escaped.

Sleeping With the Enemy

1 Samuel 27, 29, 30

One of the low points of David's life had to be the period when he lived with Israel's avowed enemies, the Philistines, for over a year. As David "slept with the enemy," he learned how compromise can give rise to three nightmares.

I. THE NIGHTMARE OF DECEIT—(1 SAMUEL 27)

A. David and his men were given refuge from Saul by Achish, the Philistine king of Gath. However, David found himself in a situation of needing to lie on a continual basis to his benefactor in order to hide his raiding activities. He protected his secret by leaving no human survivors of any city he raided.

B. "Each of you must put off falsehood and speak truthfully to his neighbor" (Ephesians 4:25). If we find ourselves compelled to lie to cover our actions, red warning lights should flash in our minds that we are living in the midst of compromise.

II. THE NIGHTMARE OF DISLOYALTY—(1 SAMUEL 29)

A. The Philistines were marching into battle against the Israelites. Irony of ironies, David, the anointed king of Israel, was marching *with* the Philistines against his own nation! David's only choice was to whom he would be disloyal—his Philistine benefactor King Achish, or his own people Israel. We'll never know what he would have done because he was sent home by untrusting Philistine generals before he reached the battlefront.

B. Jesus said, "No one can serve two masters" (Matthew 6:24) because he will hate one or the other. Sooner or later, living in a sinfully compromising situation will place us in an untenable situation where all of our choices are between what's bad and what's worse.

III. THE NIGHTMARE OF DIVISION—(1 SAMUEL 30)

A. Upon their return to Ziklag, David and his men found it burned to the ground and their loved ones all kidnapped. David's men were so bitter at the loss of their families that they "were talking of stoning him" (v. 6). Perhaps they blamed David for leading them into this dubious living arrangement among the Philistines in the first place. Fortunately for David, God rescued him and then facilitated the rescue of the hostages.

    B. "A little yeast works through the whole batch of dough" (1 Corinthians 5:6). Sinful compromise has a way of working through a business, family, or church, resulting in division and bitter recrimination. Only when we repent and return to single-minded obedience is unity restored.

CONCLUSION

"What do righteousness and wickedness have in common?" (2 Corinthians 6:14). Nothing. Don't sleep with the enemy if you want to have sweet dreams!

ILLUSTRATIONS

Staying out of untenable situations. An old sailing ship captain was asked what you do when there's a typhoon blowing and a reef to leeward. His answer, "What you do is not get yourself in that position."

Trying to please everyone. Opening speech by Gary Trudeau, the "Doonesbury" cartoonist, at Yale University's Class Day: "Dean Kagan, distinguished faculty, parents, friends, graduating seniors, Secret Service agents, class agents, people of class, people of color, colorful people, people of height, the vertically constrained, people of hair, the differently coifed, the optically challenged, the temporarily sighted, the insightful, the out of sight, the out-of-towners, the Eurocentrics, the Afrocentrics, the Afrocentrics with Eurail passes, the animal companions, friends of the earth, friends of the boss, the temporarily employed, the differently employed, the home boys, the homeless, the temporarily housed at home, and God save us, the permanently housed at home."

Low points. A reporter conducting a tedious interview with musical-comedy librettist Abe Burrows finally inquired, "Mr. Burrows, what was the low point of your life?" "I hate to say so, kid," Burrows replied, "but I think this is it."

The Lord's Anointed

2 Samuel 1:1–2:7

To David, the king of the Israelite nation wasn't just a leader, he was "The Lord's anointed." His actions in this tragic episode illustrate how Christians can implement Paul's charge to "honor men" who give themselves to servant-leadership (Philippians 2:29).

I. REGRET (1:11, 12)

A. Upon hearing of Saul and Jonathan's death in battle, David and his men mourned, tearing their clothes, weeping and fasting until evening.

B. When misfortune befalls one of our leaders in the church, we honor him or her by demonstrating our sympathy and regret. "If one part suffers, every part suffers with it" (1 Corinthians 12:26).

II. REDRESS (1:13-16)

A. The young Amalekite who brought David word of Saul's death was also the one who had finished him off. He described it as an act of mercy at Saul's request. David viewed this killing as a sin against the Lord's anointed and executed him for it.

B. Sometimes our church leaders are unjustly attacked. In those cases, faithful Christians have an obligation to move decisively to their defense (Titus 3:10). If the leader's heart and spirit are wounded then the wrong should be redressed and steps taken to make them right (Galatians 6:2).

III. RESPECT (1:17-27)

A. David wrote a beautiful song lamenting the death of Saul and Jonathan. He ordered that it be taught to the men of Judah. David's respect for the Lord's anointed is reflected in the song: "Saul and Jonathan—in life they were loved and gracious, and in death they were not parted. They were swifter than eagles, they were stronger than lions" (1:23).

B. We honor our Christian leaders by showing them respect. Instead of making jokes at their expense or disparaging their work, our words should communicate great esteem and genuine love. "Give everyone what you owe him: If you owe . . . respect, then respect" (Romans 13:7).

IV. REPLACE (2:1-4)

A. After a proper period of time, David returned to Judah to resume his rightful place on the throne. "The men of Judah came to Hebron and there they anointed David king" (2:4). How appropriate that he who showed the greatest deference to Saul, "the Lord's anointed," should follow him in that place of honor.

B. One of the greatest compliments we can pay to our church leaders is to follow in their footsteps and become the next generation of Christian leaders. "Remember your leaders, who spoke the word of God to you. Consider the outcome of their way of life and imitate their faith" (Hebrews 13:7).

V. REWARD (2:4-7)

A. Certain men of the tribe of Jabesh Gilead had honored Saul by giving his mutilated body a decent burial. When David learned this he sent word to them that he would personally reward their kindness as well as pray God's blessing upon them.

B. There is a blessed reward in store for anyone who respects, honors, and upholds the servant-leaders of the Lord's church. "Anyone who receives a righteous man because he is a righteous man will receive a righteous man's reward" (Matthew 10:41).

CONCLUSION

Ultimately "the Lord's anointed" is Jesus Christ, for that is what Christ means. To him be all the glory.

ILLUSTRATIONS

The need to replace leaders. "I am an interim preacher—and you are all interim members!"

The power of encouragement. In a recent survey of workers across the United States, nearly 85% said that they could work harder on the job. More than half claimed they could double their effectiveness "if they wanted to."

Changing of the Guard
2 Samuel 3–5

Saul died and David became the king over Israel. But it wasn't easy. Change never is. Studying David's approach to transition can help all of us better manage the changes that are inevitable in our lives. We find four principles for managing change found in David's example.

I. RESPECT FOR THE OLD (3:35-37)

A. The tribe of Judah immediately accepted David as their new leader. The rest of Israel did not. They were led by Saul's son Ish-Bosheth and the powerful general Abner. When these two had a falling out Abner made peaceful overtures toward David which David wisely accepted. However, before Abner could deliver on his promises he was treacherously murdered by David's general Joab. David took pains to show respect to the old guard by publicly rebuking Joab and mourning Abner. The effect was profound: "All the people took note and were pleased" (3:36).

B. The Bible teaches that we are to respect our elders (1 Peter 5:5). Every new generation of church leadership receives the baton from the past generation of leaders. Wisdom dictates that great sensitivity be shown to those whose influence or responsibility may be fading.

II. CONFESSION OF THE WEAK (3:38, 39)

A. David's general was responsible for Abner's murder and David could have easily shared guilt by association. But, in a disarming display of humility, David confesses his inability to control this violent man: "Today, though I am the anointed king, I am weak, and these sons of Zeruiah are too strong for me" (3:39).

B. Being human, all leaders have weaknesses. People know this to be true and expect mistakes to be made. What many people do not expect is to find a leader who is wise enough to discern his weaknesses and humble enough to admit them. That is so refreshingly rare, that the result will be *increased* acceptance of the leader and his initiatives.

III. PATIENCE WITH THE SLOW (5:4, 5)

A. At the age of thirty David was anointed king over Judah, but he had to wait seven more years before being recognized as king over the rest of Israel. Decades before, he had been anointed by Samuel the prophet and received God's promise that he would follow Saul. Nevertheless, David waited patiently and faithfully for God to bring the people's hearts over to him.

B. New leaders want to bring about the changes that they are convinced are necessary and in God's will. However, followers are sometimes wedded to old ways and alliances and are slow to accept change. Patience is required of all parties in the midst of transition, but especially of leaders, who by definition are "out front," and must often wait for the others to catch up. Allow time for the rest of the congregation to think, pray, and process the new leaders and new methods.

IV. UNION WITH THE STRONG (5:3)

A. After the death of Ish-Bosheth the elders of Israel finally came around to submit themselves to David's leadership. At that time "the king made a compact with them at Hebron before the Lord, and they anointed David the king over Israel." David's gracious spirit encouraged such unity and resulted in a period of unprecedented growth and strength for the fledgling nation.

B. There is strength in unity: "Make every effort to keep the unity of the Spirit through the bond of peace" (Ephesians 4:3). New leadership that respects the old guard, admits to weaknesses, and is patient with the slow, in God's time will experience congregational unity. This will be a period that God blesses with growth and strength.

ILLUSTRATIONS

Inevitable change. Trying to manage your life or your organization in a world changing rapidly is like dancing with a gorilla. You don't stop when you get tired. You stop when the gorilla gets tired.

Humility necessary due to mistakes in leadership. As Gib Lewis said after being introduced as the new Texas Speaker of the House, "I'm filled with humidity."

Handle With Care

2 Samuel 6; 1 Chronicles 13–15

David's attempt to bring the ark of the covenant to Jerusalem reveals both the positive *and negative* potential of zeal. It all depends upon the ingredients with which we mix our zeal. We see four examples of this in today's text.

I. ZEAL + DESIRE = PURPOSE (1 CHRONICLES 13:1-6)

A. David was zealous in his desire to be close to God: "O God . . . earnestly I seek you; my soul thirsts for you, my body longs for you" (Psalm 63:1). The ark of the covenant was where God was "enthroned between the cherubim" (13:6). David wanted that symbol of God's presence to be with him in Jerusalem.

B. God created all people with a spiritual desire, what some have called the "God-shaped vacuum." Millions are involved in a variety of spiritual quests today, but it all arises from a zealous desire to satisfy an innate spiritual hunger for God.

II. ZEAL + IGNORANCE = DEATH (1 CHRONICLES 13:7-10)

A. God had told Moses that *only Levites* were allowed to touch the ark. Moses wrote that down in Deuteronomy 10:8. David failed to follow those instructions, and as a result, Uzzah, who was not a Levite, touched the ark to steady it on its rolling cart. God struck Uzzah dead.

B. Although people may be sincere in their zeal for spiritual things, if that zeal is coupled with falsehood instead of the truth, then it will lead to death instead of life: "They are zealous for God, but their zeal is not based on knowledge" (Romans 10:2).

III. ZEAL + KNOWLEDGE = JOY (1 CHRONICLES 15:25)

A. This time David had done his homework. A beautiful scene of joy and celebration is painted as David and the Israelites dance before the ark of the covenant as it is successfully carried *on poles* (Numbers 4:14, 15), *by the Levites* (Deuteronomy 10:8) to Jerusalem.

B. God has revealed his will to us in his Word. He has given instruction for our home lives, sexual relations, church organization, and, most importantly, salvation. To the degree that we zealously follow his Word in these areas we will experience fulfillment of purpose, life, and joy.

IV. ZEAL + JEALOUSY = DIVISION (2 SAMUEL 6:16-23)

A. David's wife Michal witnessed David's expression of holy zeal and despised him for it. There seems to have been some jealousy in her reaction (6:20). David defended his zeal as being "before the Lord" and vowed to continue. This matter apparently drove a final wedge of alienation between David and Michal as the chapter ends on a somber note: "Michael . . . had no children to the day of her death" (6:23).

B. God warns us not to be unequally yoked with unbelievers and Jesus cautioned that discipleship could come between some families (Matthew 10:34). Sometimes the price of holy zeal is alienation from a jealous family member who doesn't share Christian values or spiritual fervor.

CONCLUSION

If we do pay a price for spiritual zeal, it is worth it. "Never be lacking in zeal, but keep your spiritual fervor, serving the Lord" (Romans 12:11).

ILLUSTRATION

Mistaken zeal. Noted British journalist Auburn Waugh was accustomed to receiving lecture invitations, but this one seemed a little odd: A Senegalese magazine had invited him to go to Dakar to deliver a lecture on breast-feeding. Breast-feeding? It seemed like an odd topic, since he ordinarily wrote and spoke on political topics. But they were offering him a free trip to Senegal, so he accepted. He worked feverishly upon his speech on this new subject. He arrived in Senegal at the lecture site and began his speech. It was a "passionate argument, against the practice of breast-feeding," as he later recalled in his memoirs. The audience of journalists, diplomats, and Senegalese officials looked surprised. It wasn't until later that he learned that the speech topic had somehow gotten garbled in the translation. It wasn't "breast-feeding" he should have been addressing, but "*press freedom.*"

When God Says "No"

2 Samuel 7

Someone said, "If you don't get everything you want, think of the things you *don't* get that you *don't* want!" Most of us don't like to be told "no," not even by God. David aspired to build a temple for the Lord, and the Lord told him "no." But we find David rejoicing in God's answer. How can this be? Here are three insights on how to rejoice even when God says "No."

I. REJOICE IN WHAT GOD HAS DONE (vv. 8, 9).

A. In saying "no," God reminded David of past blessings. God was responsible for David's rise from humble shepherd to king over all Israel. God had been with David wherever he went and had cut off all David's enemies. When David heard this, he heartily concurred and rejoiced in the memory: "Who am I, O Sovereign Lord, and what is my family, that you have brought me this far?" (v. 18).

B. When God says "no" to our request, we can still rejoice by remembering all of the blessings God has showered upon us in the past. "What do you have that you did not receive?" (1 Corinthians 4:7). "Praise be to the God and Father of our Lord Jesus Christ, who has blessed us in the heavenly realms with every spiritual blessing in Christ" (Ephesians 1:3).

II. REJOICE IN WHAT GOD WILL DO (vv. 9-16).

A. In saying "no," God informed David of the blessings that he had in store for him in the future. Specifically, that he would make David's name great, establish the nation of Israel, and most importantly to David, raise up his son to build God's temple and establish God's throne forever. David rejoiced, "Your words are trustworthy, and you have promised these good things to your servant" (v. 28).

B. When God says "no" to our request, we can still rejoice by reflecting on all that God has promised to do for us in the future. He has promised us a future home (John 14:2), a future body (1 Corinthians 15:42), and a future reward (1 Corinthians 3:14). Who can become bitter at a present limitation when we look forward to eternal life with God in Heaven?

III. REJOICE IN WHAT GOD IS LIKE (vv. 22, 23).

A. David praised God for who he is: "How great you are, O Sovereign Lord! There is no one *like* you, and there is no God but you." David's manner of praise was to call to God's attention the characteristics and qualities that David admired and treasured. David praised God for his greatness, sovereignty, and uniqueness (v. 22), his redemption (v. 23), his might (v. 26), and his divinity and trustworthiness (v. 28).

B. Even when God says "no" to our request, we have cause to rejoice in what our God is like. We know from experience and revelation that when we do not understand God's actions, we can *always* trust his heart. The purpose of prayer is not just to get things, it is to communicate with God himself. Our goal is to become the best worshipers of God that we can possibly be. "I pray that you . . . may be filled to the measure of all the fullness of God" (Ephesians 3:17, 19).

ILLUSTRATION

Resent being told "no" or what to do. A banker was approached on the street by a seedy-looking character with the shakes, asking for a handout. He reached into his pocket and pressed a bill into the man's hand. "Now don't waste this on booze. See to it that you get some good food," he said. The seedy recipient replied, "My dear sir, do I tell you what to do with *your* money?"

The Heart of God

2 Samuel 9, 21

Just as X rays pass through the human body and reveal an accurate picture of the heart to the physician's trained eye, there were some important ways in which the actions of David revealed the heart of God. We get one of those X rays in the remarkable story of Mephibosheth.

I. WE SEE GOD'S HEART IN THE MERCIFUL QUEST (9:3).

A. After David became king, he went on a mission of mercy, searching for a surviving relative of Saul so that he could show him a kindness.

B. David's merciful quest reveals the heart of God. God is a missionary. The Bible tells the story of a God on a quest to show mercy to the "house of Adam."

II. WE SEE GOD'S HEART IN THE OBJECT OF DAVID'S MERCY (9:3-6).

A. Mephibosheth was crippled in both feet—Man is handicapped by sin, incapable of journeying to Heaven without help (Hebrews 12:12, 13).

B. Mephibosheth was the grandson of the former king, a potential rival to the throne—Man is a rival to God's throne, and every sin is an attempt to take God's place (Ephesians 2:3).

C. Mephibosheth was an orphan—Man is a spiritual orphan. Paul says that before we became Christians we had no promise, no Christ, no God, and no hope (Ephesians 2:12).

III. WE SEE GOD'S HEART IN THE BASIS OF SALVATION (9:7).

A. Mephibosheth was saved because he and David had a mutual relationship to Jonathan, Mephibosheth's father. Mephibosheth was shown kindness for Jonathan's sake.

B. Because of the love of the Father, Jesus was sent to die for the sins of the world. Those whom God saves, he saves because of their relationship to his Son Jesus. "He who loves me will be loved by my Father, and I too will love him" (John 14:21).

IV. WE SEE GOD'S HEART IN THE ADOPTION AND REWARD (9:7-11).

A. Mephibosheth was given the land and possessions of his grandfather King Saul. Likewise, Christians are the recipients of a great inheritance. "We are ... heirs of God and co-heirs with Christ" (Romans 8:17).

B. Mephibosheth was invited to be a regular at the table of the king. The last part of verse 11 says that he became like one of the king's own sons. Likewise, Christians are seated at the table of the King. Every Sunday we gather in the church and partake of the Lord's Supper at the Lord's table, and the King, though invisible, is present (Matthew 26:29).

V. WE SEE GOD'S HEART IN THE ESCAPE FROM DEATH (21:5-7).

A. In this chapter there is a brief but interesting postscript to the story. Saul had unjustly made war against the Gibeonites and as a result God struck Israel with famine in David's reign. David asked the Gibeonites what he could do to appease them and thereby end the famine. Their reply was to demand seven men from the descendants of Saul to hang. David handed them over. He gave them seven grandsons of Saul and they were hanged—but he refused to give them Mephibosheth because, the Bible says, of Jonathan.

B. On the day of judgment the books will be opened with the records of our lives and we will be confronted with the evidence that we are guilty and deserving of death. But the people of faith will have an advocate, a defender, who is Jesus Christ. For the sake of Jesus, God will spare our lives.

ILLUSTRATION

Loving for the sake of another. In the summer I like to take my two children, Stephen and Katie, fishing to a nearby lake. I take them because I love them. And whoever happens to be over at our house playing with them when I announce a fishing trip is automatically invited. I take them all. Why? Obviously, it's because they're friends of my children. That's their ticket to ride. When I love my kids there's a little extra love to slosh over onto whoever happens to be with them at the time.

Try a Little Kindness
2 Samuel 10

Kindness is a misunderstood virtue today. Many believe they are being kind when they simply tolerate someone else. Others see kindness as allowing others to trample our feelings.

David was a man of kindness, but he did not fit those definitions. Here we see the characteristics of true kindness.

I. KINDNESS IS MEMORABLE (vv. 1, 2).
A. David's act of kindness was spawned by a kindness done to him by Nahash, king of the Ammonites, that left a deep and favorable impression.

B. When someone does a kindness for us we tend to remember. Be kind to others and they will never forget you. "You always have pleasant memories of us" (1 Thessalonians 3:6).

II. KINDNESS IS SYMPATHETIC (vv. 1, 2).
A. When Nahash died David sent a delegation to his son "to express his sympathy to Hanun concerning his father." David wasn't too busy to take time out to sympathize with a grief-stricken foreign king.

B. The death of a parent is one of the most difficult times for anyone. It is important that Christians seize the opportunity to minister in kindness by demonstrating sympathy in a tangible way, i.e., cards, phone calls, or personal visits. "We can comfort those in any trouble with the comfort we ourselves have received from God" (2 Corinthians 1:4).

III. KINDNESS IS VULNERABLE (vv. 2-4).
A. David's delegation of sympathy was not well received. The Ammonites suspicions poisoned their thinking and caused them to misinterpret David's overture as an act of espionage. They humiliated David's ambassadors by shaving half their beards and cutting off their clothes at the waist. Then they were sent home.

B. The sad fact is that kindness is not *always* returned by kindness. Our sinful nature can cause us to be suspicious and misinterpret good intentions. We are kind in obedience to God, not because it always "pays off." "He is kind to the ungrateful and wicked" (Luke 6:35).

IV. KINDNESS IS SENSITIVE (v. 5).
A. David's delegation was "greatly humiliated." When David found out, he did something remarkably sensitive. He had them stay in Jericho until their beards could grow back out. That way they could come home and enter Jerusalem with their dignity in tact.

B. When people go through periods of humiliation or embarrassment, sometimes we are in a position to ease the way. A kind person is sensitive to the feelings of others and attempts to help them save face whenever possible. "Love . . . always protects" (1 Corinthians 13:6, 7).

V. KINDNESS IS STRONG (vv. 6-19).
A. The Ammonites continued to make a bad situation worse. Worried about attack from David, they hired twenty thousand Aramean mercenaries. When David saw them making battle preparations he attacked and defeated them. David's kindness was not weakness, as shown by his military strength. David's kindness was simply an expression of a different kind of strength, strength of character.

B. Some mistakenly think that a man who is sympathetic, sensitive, and kind is somehow weak. The Bible teaches that just the opposite is true. Kindness is an expression of strength and can be a powerful weapon for good. "Overcome evil with good" (Romans 12:21).

ILLUSTRATION
People who don't care. Robert Henry went shopping in a large discount store, hoping to purchase a pair of binoculars. As he walked up to the appropriate counter, he noticed that he was the only customer in the store. The counter person looked up at him and said, "You got a number?" "I got a what?" asked Robert, trying to control his astonishment. "You got a number? You gotta have a number." So, he went to the take-a-number machine, pulled number 37, and walked back to the salesperson. Her number counter revealed that the last customer waited on had been number 34. So she screamed out "35! . . . 35! . . . 36! . . . 36! . . . 37!" "I'm number 37," said Robert. "May I help you?" she asked without cracking a smile. "No," replied Robert, and he turned around and walked out.—From *How to Win Customers and Keep Them for Life*, by Michael LeBouf.

Prepped for Disaster
2 Samuel 11:1-4

David's own unwise actions placed him in a position of vulnerability to temptation. Four distinct steps David took led him down the road to disaster. We can take note and avoid the same mistakes.

I. NEGLIGENCE (v. 1)

A. David neglected his duties as king. The sacred record states that spring was the time when kings went off to war. Nevertheless, David sent Joab out with the army while "David remained in Jerusalem." If David had been performing his official duties as king, he would not have experienced this particular temptation.

B. All Christians have certain responsibilities that are uniquely theirs. Those duties may include motherhood, fatherhood, job, school, church leadership, and service in ministry among other things. When we faithfully perform those responsibilities we remain in God's will: "A man who walks by day will not stumble" (John 11:9). When we neglect our duties we step out of God's will and into the line of fire, Satan's fire.

II. IDLENESS (v. 2)

A. David got up from his bed one evening and walked around on the roof of his palace. Why couldn't he sleep? A reasonable inference is that he couldn't sleep because he had been spending his days in idleness. "The sleep of a laborer is sweet" (Ecclesiastes 5:12). If David had been leading his army in battle he would have gone to his pallet each night exhausted, unhindered by insomnia! "Idle hands are the devil's workshop" may not be inspired, but David illustrates its colloquial truth.

B. When we are idle we prep ourselves for disaster. "Warn those who are idle" (1 Thessalonians 5:14). Idleness during the day can cause sleeplessness at night and the nighttime is fraught with sexual temptation. "It is when he walks by night that he stumbles, for he has no light" (John 11:10). Not only is this true figuratively, it is often true literally as well. The safest place to be at night is *asleep* in your *own* bed with your *own* spouse.

III. CARELESSNESS (v. 2)

A. From the roof of his palace David saw a woman bathing, and the woman was very beautiful. David saw Bathsheba because of his own carelessness. Because of his negligence and idleness he was at the wrong place at the wrong time, and he saw what he never should have seen.

B. Christians, and especially men, have an obligation to guard their eyes. The fires of lust are fueled by what we see. "Anyone who looks at a woman lustfully has already committed adultery with her in his heart. If your right eye causes you to sin, gouge it out and throw it away" (Matthew 5:28, 29). We must not allow our carelessness to put us in the wrong place at the wrong time where we will be the most vulnerable to temptation.

IV. COVETOUSNESS (vv. 3, 4)

A. David sent messengers to find out who the woman was. The answer came back, "Bathsheba . . . the wife of Uriah the Hittite" (v. 3). As soon as David discovered that Bathsheba was married he should have discontinued his involvement. Instead, David sent messengers to get her. "You shall not covet your neighbor's wife" (Exodus 20:17).

B. Before someone actually steals the spouse of another, he or she makes the conscious, deliberate choice to nurse an unholy desire in his or her heart. God expects us to find satisfaction and contentment in the spouse that we have entered into covenant with. "Rejoice in the wife of your youth" (Proverbs 5:18).

ILLUSTRATION

Negligence & Idleness. A wealthy landowner was checking employee records and called a longtime employee into his study. "Peter," asked the billionaire real estate tycoon, "how long have you been with us now?" "Almost 25 years," replied the employee. His employer frowned. "According to these records, you were hired to take care of the stables." "That's correct, sir," said Peter. "But we haven't owned horses for more than 20 years," said his boss. "Right sir. What would you like me to do next?"

The Tangled Web— Part 1

2 Samuel 11:4-15

"Oh what a tangled web we weave when first we practice to deceive." The threads of David's sin and cover-up were woven into a deadly trap in which he was ultimately caught. Let us examine four threads of that web today.

I. THE THREAD OF ADULTERY (v. 4)

A. David sent messengers to get Bathsheba, and "he slept with her." David broke the seventh commandment, "You shall not commit adultery" (Exodus 20:14). Once David planted the seed of this sin, he, and others around him, began to reap a bitter harvest.

B. Adultery is a grave sin. All those who engage in adultery bring dire consequences upon themselves and others. "Why be captivated, my son, by an adulteress? Why embrace the bosom of another man's wife?" (Proverbs 5:20).

II. THE THREAD OF ILLEGITIMACY (v. 5)

A. After the sin, David sent Bathsheba back home, intending to go about business as usual. However, after some time had passed, Bathsheba sent David a message informing him that she had conceived his child. How would Bathsheba explain this to Uriah? What would David do about the welfare of *his* child by another man's wife?

B. It is profitable to consider the potential consequences of adultery in the sober, dispassionate climate of forethought. Think about the possibility of fathering or conceiving an illegitimate child. What of that poor child? What of the betrayed spouses? What of the lack of control, or legal rights, of the "bio-dad"? Is it worth it?

III. THE THREAD OF DUPLICITY (vv. 6-13)

A. A striking contrast in character is played out. In a devious attempt to cover his sin, David brings Uriah back from the siege of Rabbah hoping he will sleep with Bathsheba and, subsequently, think that David's child is his. But Uriah has too much integrity, refusing to indulge himself in any way while his comrades, David's soldiers, are fighting on the field.

B. Paul says that wickedness is "ever-increasing" (Romans 6:19). Here we see the evil progression of sin as David advances from sin to cover-up. In his efforts he deceitfully manipulates an innocent man of honor to cover his own misdeeds. If we indulge in sin it can harden our hearts to the point of justifying the manipulation of innocent people for our own selfish purposes.

IV. THE THREAD OF CONSPIRACY (vv. 14, 15)

A. Having been frustrated in his cover-up by Uriah's integrity, David now turns to his general Joab to do the dirty work for him. Joab is no stranger to conspiracy or murder (2 Samuel 3:27). Through a letter, ironically carried by Uriah himself, David instructs Joab to arrange for the innocent man's death in battle.

B. "You may be sure that your sin will find you out" (Numbers 32:23), but until it does, many attempt to hide it. When the consequences become too widespread for one sinner to cover, it becomes necessary to draw others into the effort, thereby corrupting them through conspiracy. "A violent man entices his neighbor and leads him down a path that is not good" (Proverbs 16:29).

CONCLUSION

David's life became tangled and complicated by his sin and attempted cover-up. There are four more sticky threads to come. Sin has the same effect in our lives today.

ILLUSTRATION

Trying to keep a deadly secret. A melon farmer's crop of melons was disappearing fast from his field. Thieves were constantly stealing the melons under the cover of night's darkness. The farmer became desperate and in an attempt to save his crop from the vandals he decided to put up a sign. The sign had on it a skull and crossbones, and it read: "One of these melons is poisoned," only the farmer knew that it was not true. Sure enough, for two nights not a melon was missing. But after the third night, the farmer noticed that his sign had been altered. Someone had scratched out the word "One" and replaced it with another word. The sign now read, "*Two* of these melons are poisoned."

The Tangled Web— Part 2

2 Samuel 11:16-27

"The evil deeds of a wicked man ensnare him; the cords of his sin hold him fast" (Proverbs 5:22). As we complete the sordid tale of David and Bathsheba, we witness the truth of this proverb. Even a powerful king cannot escape the tangled web of his own deceit. Let us examine the remaining four strands of that web today.

I. THE THREAD OF FATALITY (vv. 16, 17)

A. In obedience to David's secret written communiqué, Joab placed Uriah in a high-risk battle-zone. The desired result, Uriah's death, was achieved. Even though it was not the hand of David that did the killing, he was nevertheless guilty of murder. "You struck down Uriah the Hittite with the sword" (12:9). David was now guilty of innocent bloodshed.

B. Innocent people get hurt by sin. Sometimes that is deliberate and sometimes it is just a by-product. Jesus taught that to hold anger and contempt in one's heart for a brother is akin to murder (Matthew 5:21, 22). "The wages of sin is death" (Romans 6:23), meaning our own death. In order for us to live, an innocent man had to die: "Christ died for sins once for all, the righteous for the unrighteous" (1 Peter 3:18).

II. THE THREAD OF HYPOCRISY (vv. 18-25)

A. Joab sent David a message about the fatalities in the battle. In order to dispose of Uriah, Joab had taken unnecessary risks with the men's lives. Ordinarily this would have merited a rebuke from David, "the king's anger may flare up" (v. 20), so Joab emphasized Uriah's death. When David received the news of the unusually high casualties, he was conciliatory. "Don't let this upset you; the sword devours one as well as another" (v. 25). David's sin led to hypocritical leniency toward himself and his general.

B. Jesus' most severe rebukes were reserved for religious hypocrites (Matthew 23). Hypocrisy is a serious sin. Hypocrisy results from willful, sustained disobedience. It causes one's thinking to become so darkened that he winds up calling evil good and good evil. Hypocrites are actually pleased with the misfortune of others, if it benefits them.

III. THE THREAD OF AUDACITY (vv. 26, 27)

A. After Uriah was killed and Bathsheba had mourned, David wasted no time in bringing her to his house and making her his wife. David's audacity is remarkable. Not only does he commit adultery with another man's wife. Not only does he father an illegitimate child by her. Not only does he arrange for the woman's husband to be murdered. But after his death, he takes the widow to be his own wife. Bathsheba must now share a bed and a child with the man who murdered her husband.

B. Protracted sin hardens the heart so that the sinner is not even embarrassed or ashamed of what he has done. "Are they ashamed of their loathsome conduct? No, they have no shame at all; they do not even know how to blush" (Jeremiah 8:12).

IV. THE THREAD OF DIVINE ANIMOSITY (v. 27)

A. God knew what David had done and God was displeased. All sin is ultimately against God. In his holiness, the Lord cannot allow sin to stand unpunished. David's flaunting of God and his laws placed him in the path of the wrath of the righteous Lord.

B. No one ever "gets away" with sin. When people sin it does not escape God's notice. Sinners outside of Christ are "by nature objects of wrath" (Ephesians 2:3). Christians who sin may escape condemnation by God's grace but will still experience Divine displeasure and many unpleasant consequences. "For a man's ways are in full view of the Lord, and he examines all his paths" (Proverbs 5:21).

ILLUSTRATION

Some things are impossible to reverse. A Kentucky farmer is said to have observed, "You can't produce pigs by running the sausage machine backwards."

Audacity. I'm reminded of the Harvard University professor's prayer, "Dear Lord, please deliver us from the terrible sin of intellectual arrogance, which for your information means . . ."

Reality Check

2 Samuel 12:1-7

Sin deceives and blinds us. When caught in our web of sin, we may need extreme measures to restore our vision and balance. God used four powerful punches to bring David back to the reality of his sin and need for repentance and cleansing.

I. A PLUCKY PROPHET (v. 1)

A. The Lord sent Nathan the prophet to David. Nathan had brought glad tidings to David in the past (2 Samuel 7). On this day, however, Nathan's mission would be one of correction, requiring much courage. Nathan proved equal to the task.

B. God uses men and women of courage in our lives to deliver reality checks. Godly people with backbone and spiritual insight can be counted on to help us with our blind spots. "He who rebukes a man will in the end gain more favor than he who has a flattering tongue" (Proverbs 28:23).

II. A POIGNANT STORY (vv. 1-4)

A. Nathan used a story to penetrate David's wall of self-justification and deceit. In seven powerful sentences, Nathan told of a poor man whose one beloved pet lamb was confiscated by a rich and greedy neighbor. Immediately David's emotions were engaged and his passions aroused.

B. The poignant story is a powerful punch that God uses to deliver his reality checks. The characteristic of Jesus' teaching style most remembered is the parable. The Bible itself is a book of stories. The story is effective because, like David, we quickly identify with a main character in the story, usually the protagonist. The kicker often comes when, like David, God reveals that we have played the role of *antagonist*. At that point our defenses have been disarmed, for our emotions and passions are engaged.

III. A PASSIONATE PRONOUNCEMENT (vv. 5, 6)

A. At the conclusion of Nathan's story, David made a passionate pronouncement. He declared that the merciless rich man deserved to die and would have to make four-fold restitution to the offended poor man. Having thus gone on record, David could now be held accountable by his own words.

B. God uses passionate pronouncements as reality checks in our lives. Every Christian has stood publicly to make the "good confession." It is a statement of our belief in Jesus as Savior and submission to him as Lord. "If you confess with your mouth, 'Jesus is Lord,' and believe in your heart that God raised him from the dead, you will be saved" (Romans 10:9). When we stray into self-justification and sin, God can draw us back to such pronouncements and hold us accountable to our confession.

IV. A POINTED CONFRONTATION (v. 7)

A. "Then Nathan said to David, 'You are the man!'" God delivered his knockout punch through this pointed confrontation. Once David went on record, the prophet identified him as the offender in the story and confronted him with his adultery and murder. For the first time in months, David is forced out of his dark denial into the bright light of truth.

B. Nothing can take the place of direct confrontation for turning those who are engaged in sinful denial. Whether we are on the receiving or giving end of a confrontation, recognize it as God's great reality check.

ILLUSTRATIONS

Courage to tell the truth. Samuel Goldwyn: "I don't want any yes-men around me. I want everyone to tell me the truth even if it costs them their jobs!"

Herbert Agar: "The truth that makes men free is, for the most part, the truth which men prefer not to hear."

Pointed confrontations. As a baseball player, a coach, and a manager, Frankie Frisch never hid his lack of affection for umpires. Once, when Frisch was coaching third base, umpire Bill Klem called a runner out on a close play. Frisch screamed his own interpretation of the play. Then he put his hand to his heart and fell to the ground.

Klem calmly walked over to the fallen coach, who lay on the ground with his eyes closed. "Frisch," Klem said, "dead or alive, you're out of the game."

Rebound—Part 1

2 Samuel 12:7-13

David's experience following his sin demonstrates how to successfully rebound after a personal moral failure. Let us examine the first four steps David made.

I. COMPREHEND THE GRAVITY (vv. 7-9).

A. David listened as Nathan the prophet spelled out in painful detail the gravity of his sin. David was made to understand that he had (1) disdained God's blessings, (2) despised God's Word, (3) committed murder, and (4) committed adultery.

B. In order to rebound after personal moral failure it is essential that we understand the gravity of our sin. The ugliness of our sin must be impressed upon our hearts in order for true repentance, restitution, and restoration to take place. Then and only then will we "Hate what is evil; cling to what is good" (Romans 12:9).

II. FACE THE CONSEQUENCES (vv. 10-14).

A. Nathan continues by enumerating the consequences of David's sin. These include (1) perennial violence in David's house, (2) the ravaging of David's wives, (3) humiliation before David's public, and (4) the death of David's child.

B. The consequences of sin are always painful. Suffering results from many different causes; but some of our suffering, if we're honest, is the direct result of our own sin. In forcing us to face the devastating consequences of our sin, God can build a resolve within our spirit to win the fight against temptation the next time.

III. ACKNOWLEDGE RESPONSIBILITY (v. 13).

A. A turning point arrived for David when he said flatly, "I have sinned against the Lord." Having comprehended the gravity and faced up to the consequences of his sin, David took full responsibility for what he had done. He made no excuses and laid no blame.

B. No sinner can be forgiven until he acknowledges that he is a sinner and is responsible for acts of rebellion against God and his righteous laws. Many in our society attempt to shirk responsibility for misdeeds, but that will never stand before the Lord. "All have sinned and fall short of the glory of God" (Romans 3:23). "If we claim to be without sin, we deceive ourselves and the truth is not in us" (1 John 1:8).

IV. ACCEPT GOD'S MERCY (v. 13).

A. Finally, Nathan speaks of God's mercy. "The Lord has taken away your sin. You are not going to die." Some fail to understand that forgiveness and consequences co-exist. Even though David faced many *temporal* consequences for his sin, he would suffer no *eternal* consequences. David's sin was grievous, however, "where sin increased, grace increased all the more" (Romans 5:20).

B. In order to rebound following a moral failure, it is imperative that we accept God's mercy. The Lord has taken away *our* sin too. Sometimes people do not rebound because they cannot seem to forgive *themselves* for their failure. If God has forgiven us, we can forgive ourselves. God's mercy is made possible by Jesus' death. That is what the cross was all about.

CONCLUSION

David rebounded from terrible moral failure and sin. If David could rebound and still be used mightily by God, so can we.

ILLUSTRATIONS

What goes around comes around. When a three-year-old son opened the birthday gift from his grandmother, he discovered a water pistol. He squealed with delight and headed for the nearest sink. His mother was not so pleased. She turned to her mom and said, "I'm surprised at you. Don't you remember how we used to drive you crazy with water guns?" Her mom smiled and replied, "I remember."

Consequences. It's better to be known by six people for something you're proud of than by six million for something you're not.

Taking responsibility. "The problem with the world today is that no one wants to take responsibility for anything . . . but don't quote me on that!"

Rebound—Part 2

2 Samuel 12:14-31

David's experience demonstrates how to rebound after a personal moral failure. Four steps were reviewed last time. Four more steps are presented here.

I. LIVE WITH HOPE (vv. 14-23).

   A. Nathan had pronounced God's judgment against David for his sin. That judgment included the death of David and Bathsheba's son. Nevertheless, David fasted and prayed for seven days, interceding on the boy's behalf. The child died on the seventh day. David explained his source of hope: "I thought, 'Who knows? The Lord may be gracious to me and let the child live'" (v. 22).

   B. Though we must live with the consequences of our sin, that doesn't mean that they are always permanent or irreversible. Taking into consideration the gracious character of the Lord, we can continue to hope and pray for mercy whether it takes seven days, seven years, or seven decades. Who knows? The Lord may be gracious to us!

II. WALK BY FAITH (vv. 20, 23).

   A. In all of the tragedy David experienced, he did not lose his faith. Two steps illustrate his faith-walk. (1) After the child died, David went into the house of the Lord and worshiped. (2) His testimony to his servants about the afterlife —"I will go to him, but he will not return to me" (v. 23). Even in grief David trusted the Lord.

   B. As time goes by we may forget that many of our wounds are self-inflicted. That's when we're tempted to blame God. To rebound fully we must continue to place our trust in him through worship and a confident expectation of future reward in Heaven.

III. GROW IN LOVE (vv. 24, 25).

   A. These two verses are crowded with love. David loved Bathsheba and comforted her. They conceived another child whom they named Solomon, and the Lord loved him. The Lord loved Solomon so much that he dubbed him Jedidiah, which means "loved by the Lord."

B. It is not what happens *to* us that is most important but what happens *in* us. Out of the same tragedy can come regression or progression, isolation or outreach, hate or love, the choice is always ours. We must consciously embrace love for family, church, God, and neighbor. In this way we "fall forward."

IV. RETURN TO GOOD WORKS (vv. 26-31).

A. David's troubles started when he neglected his proper duties by not leading the army in war. Here we find Joab encouraging David to return to the battlefield to lead the final action of the military campaign against the Ammonites. David successfully led the army to victory and was crowned with gold and jewels. He was back in the saddle again.

B. Having faced the consequences, including any time of mandated probation, we rebound from moral failure by returning to work, service, and ministry for God. God has no perfect ministers, only forgiven ones. We were "created in Christ Jesus to do good works" (Ephesians 2:10). In his great service we will find our ultimate renewal and restoration.

CONCLUSION

We must never allow Satan to convince us that we can't make a comeback. We can, and God helping us, we will. David proves it.

ILLUSTRATION

Overcoming obstacles by faith and hope. Ten-year-old Danny Wiello, tragically lost his left arm in an auto accident. His therapist, a Judo student, began to show him some of the conditioning used in the Judo training. Soon, Danny began to train with his therapist's Japanese Judo master. After many months the other boys in Danny's group signed up for a regional tournament. Danny signed up too. The master taught the other boys many special moves, but taught Danny only one new move. On the day of the tournament, Danny won all of his matches. He even pinned the previous year's champion. In the car on the way home, Danny asked how the Master knew that he could win with his one special move. The master smiled and said, "The only known defense for that move is for your opponent to grab your *left* arm."

Paean to Forgiveness
Psalm 32

David celebrated forgiveness in this Psalm following the exposure of his sin with Bathsheba. Here we find five distinctive notes in the melody of God's mercy.

I. THE BLESSING OF FORGIVENESS (vv. 1, 2)

A. In this passage there are several phrases that describe God's forgiveness in wonderful ways. "Forgiven" means *to lift off or take away.* "Covered" means *to conceal with a lid or veil; to put out of sight.* "Not count against him" means *a complete and entire acquittal.*

B. The Hebrew word for "blessed" could be paraphrased, "Oh, the happiness many times over!" There are multiplied benefits for those who gain true forgiveness of sins from God on his terms.

II. THE ALTERNATIVE TO FORGIVENESS (vv. 3, 4)

A. David shows how he felt during the months of cover-up following his drastic sin with Bathsheba and before God's condemnation of that sin through the prophet Nathan. David was "wasted away" and "groaning all day long." He felt the hand of God "heavy upon me." His strength was drained as in the "heat of summer."

B. Sin brings guilt that causes us to go through inner torment and anguish. The secrecy of the sin and its consequences only add to the distress and feed the downward spiral of condemnation and self-loathing.

III. THE PATHWAY TO FORGIVENESS (v. 5)

A. David's pathway to forgiveness was found in an acknowledgment of sin before God and abandonment of the cover-up. "Then I acknowledged my sin to you and did not cover up my iniquity."

B. John assures Christians that there is forgiveness afforded to those who will confess their sins to the Lord (1 John 1:9). To confess is literally to "say the same as." Confession means that we agree with God that our action was wrong. Confession to another person (as did David to Nathan) can help break the addictive power of some sins.

IV. THE ASSURANCE OF FORGIVENESS (vv. 5-7)

A. David expresses his assurance that the Lord "forgave the guilt of my sin" (v. 5). He uses figures of speech to communicate the reliability of God's mercy. God is the safe and dry high ground in a flood (v. 6) and the "hiding place" of protection and deliverance (v. 7).

B. Even Christians are sometimes in need of assurance that their sins are forgiven. David helps us to remember that the assurance of our forgiveness is founded upon God's trustworthiness, not our consistency. "Let God be true, and every man a liar" (Romans 3:4).

V. THE TESTIMONY OF FORGIVENESS (vv. 8-11)

A. David concludes with a testimony about the forgiveness of God. Now that he has learned the hard way he would instruct others "in the way you should go" (v. 8). He warns against mule-like stubborn resistance to God's way that only leads to many woes.

B. Every Christian has a testimony to share—a testimony of our own forgiveness. It's not enough to receive God's mercy for ourselves; we are obligated to instruct others so as to enlarge the circle of worshipers who can "rejoice in the Lord and be glad" (v. 11).

ILLUSTRATION

Secret falsehoods. In the Wild West days of outlaws and desperadoes, a name stood out above all the rest, Black Bart. During his reign of terror, he is credited with stealing the bags and breath away from 29 different stagecoach crews. A hood hid his face, no victims ever saw him, no sheriff could ever track his trail, no shots were fired, nor did he ever take a hostage. He didn't have to—his presence was enough to paralyze. As it turns out, he wasn't anything to be afraid of. When the authorities finally tracked down the thief, they found a mild-mannered druggist from Decatur, Illinois. A man who was so afraid of horses that he rode to and from his robberies in a buggy. He was Charles E. Bowles, the bandit who never fired a shot because he never once loaded his gun. Any falsehoods in your world?

Reconciliation

2 Samuel 13, 14

David's reconciliation with Absalom provides a model for Christian reconciliation. In our text for today can be found six principles for bringing conflicting parties back together.

I. THE DIFFICULTY OF RECONCILIATION (2 SAMUEL 13)

A. 2 Samuel 13 records that David became estranged from his son Absalom when Absalom murdered his own brother, Amnon, for raping Absalom's sister, Tamar. Absalom fled to Geshur where he lived in exile for three years.

B. The difficulty of reconciliation is that the initial cause of estrangement is often based on a very real injustice. When we, or someone we love, is harmed by another, our feelings are hurt and a wall of outrage is erected. Such walls are high, thick, and not easily breached.

II. THE NEED FOR RECONCILIATION (13:39)

A. As time passed, David was consoled concerning Amnon's death, and "the spirit of the king longed to go to Absalom." David had a strong desire to be reconciled to his son, but at this point, his pride continued to bar the way.

B. God has created us for fellowship and unity, especially with members of our own family. When that fellowship is interrupted, we experience a longing for its restoration. We need reconciliation to salve the pangs of loneliness and feed the hunger for companionship.

III. THE AMBASSADORS OF RECONCILIATION (14:1-20)

A. Joab, in cooperation with a wise woman from Tekoa, interceded with David on Absalom's behalf to convince him to allow Absalom to return to Jerusalem. The woman used a story to penetrate David's heart, much as the prophet Nathan had done earlier.

B. Many times reconciliation depends upon the willingness and availability of an objective third party who will act as peacemaker between two estranged people. God calls Christians to such a ministry. "Blessed are the peacemakers" (Matthew 5:9).

IV. THE MANDATE FOR RECONCILIATION (14:14)

A. "God . . . devises ways so that a banished person may not remain estranged from him." What a powerful statement about the heart and conduct of God. As a "man after God's own heart," how can David object to the proposal for reconciliation with Absalom?

B. The mandate for reconciliation is found in God's own nature. God devised a plan (the cross) by which sinful man could be reconciled to him. We are to "be imitators of God" (Ephesians 5:1).

V. THE RIGORS OF RECONCILIATION (14:24-32)

A. Even after David consented to allow Absalom back into Jerusalem, he refused to see him in person for another two years.

B. Reconciliation is a rigorous process. It doesn't often happen all at once. The walls of pain, anger, and pride take *time* to come down. Patience, persistence, and perseverance are required to accomplish the goal.

VI. THE FRUIT OF RECONCILIATION (14:33)

A. Finally, after two years and further intervention by Joab, David allowed Absalom into his presence and kissed him. The reconciliation of father and son was complete.

B. The fruit of reconciliation is worth the effort that is required in the rigorous process. It is the sweet fruit of a restored fellowship and freedom from the prison of bitterness. "There is . . . joy for those who promote peace" (Proverbs 12:20).

ILLUSTRATION

Burying the hatchet. Joe was on his sickbed and seemed close to death. For years he had been at odds with his one-time best friend, Steve. Finally, he summoned Steve to his room and confessed that he was afraid to meet God with an unresolved grudge in his life. So, slowly and with great difficulty he apologized to Steve for all of the bad thoughts he'd had and the bad words he'd said about Steve. As Steve turned to go, however, Joe said, "Now remember, if I get well again, none of this counts!" Some people want to bury the hatchet but *leave the handle sticking out.*

When the Bottom Falls Out

2 Samuel 15

The bottom fell out of David's world when his own son Absalom conspired to usurp his throne. David's actions demonstrate how we can cope when the bottom falls out of our world. Let us consider these five steps in confronting calamity.

I. RETREAT (vv. 13, 14)

A. When David received news that "the hearts of the men of Israel are with Absalom," he ordered the immediate evacuation of those who were loyal to him in the city. Thus began a desperate retreat toward the desert.

B. When disaster strikes, one of the best initial reactions we can take is to retreat toward the desert. In Scripture the desert is often used to represent a place of God's special care: "I cared for you in the desert" (Hosea 13:5).

II. RECEIVE (vv. 19-22)

A. David placed no demands upon others when his crisis came: "Why should you come along with us?" (v. 19). However, friends like Ittai the Gittite offered their support, "Wherever my lord the king may be, whether it means life or death, there will your servant be" (v. 21). David gratefully received their support (v. 22).

B. When the bottom falls out for us, Christian friends will want to help and will offer to help. *Receiving* help from friends in times of trouble is just as important as offering it. "Unless I wash you, you have no part with me" (John 13:8).

III. RELEASE (vv. 24-26)

A. David released control over the ark of the covenant by sending it back to Jerusalem with Zadok the priest. The ark represented the very presence of God. In this action, David released his fate to the sovereignty of God saying, "I am ready; let him do to me whatever seems good to him" (v. 26).

B. When the bottom falls out we must remember that there are so many things beyond the reach of our control. We must release ourselves to the sovereignty of a good and just God. "Therefore do not worry about tomorrow" (Matthew 6:34).

IV. REPENT (v. 30)

A. As David fled the city he was repenting, "weeping as he went; his head was covered, and he was barefoot." In the midst of his tragedy, David wasn't blaming God, rather he was humbling himself before God and seeking his face.

B. Whether we believe our suffering is the result of our own sin or not, it is always a good idea to turn to God in humility and repentance in times of crises. When the bottom falls out we only have two choices, turn toward God or turn away from God. To repent means to turn—let the direction of that turn always be *toward* God. "Your sorrow led you to repentance" (2 Corinthians 7:9).

V. RETRENCH (vv. 31-37)

A. Even though David was in retreat, he had not given up. He prayed, asking God to frustrate his enemies (v. 31). He also sent Hushai, Zadok, and Abiathar back into the city for intelligence and subterfuge.

B. While the bottom is falling out is no time to give up. We retrench by trusting God and fighting the enemy with the spiritual weapons at our disposal. "Therefore we do not lose heart. Though outwardly we are wasting away, yet inwardly we are being renewed day by day" (2 Corinthians 4:16).

CONCLUSION

When the bottom fell out for David, the Lord was there to catch him. God is our safety net as well, if we have the faith to trust him.

ILLUSTRATION

When the bottom falls out. The photographer for a national magazine was assigned to shoot a great forest fire. He was told that a small plane would be waiting to take him over the fire. He arrived at the airstrip just an hour before sundown. Sure enough, the Cessna was waiting. He jumped in with his equipment and shouted, "Let's go!" The pilot swung the plane into the wind and soon they were in the air. "Fly over the north side of the fire," said the photographer, "and make several low-level passes." "Why?" asked the nervous pilot. "Because I'm going to take pictures!" retorted the photographer. "I'm a photographer, and photographers take pictures." After a long pause, the pilot replied, "You mean, you're not the instructor?"

Turn the Other Cheek
2 Samuel 16:5-14; 19:18-23

One thousand years before Jesus taught "turn the other cheek," David was doing it. David's example encourages us to do likewise. Let us examine this story to learn how to react to such unfair attacks.

I. PROFILE OF A SLAPPER (v. 5)

A. The "slapper" in this story is a man named Shimei. Shimei was a member of the clan of Saul the former king. He seems to have held a grudge against David for succeeding Saul as king of Israel. In his hatred, he heaps rocks and insults upon David and his companions as they retreat from Jerusalem.

B. People become "slappers" for all kinds of reasons. They may be jealous of our success. They may have had mean-spirited parents, and that's all they know. Their slaps may be an expression of their own misery. Turning the other cheek might be more possible if we try to put ourselves in the "slappers" shoes.

II. ANATOMY OF A SLAP (vv. 6-8)

A. Slaps are insulting. Shimei knew all the right buttons to push. He chided David for being a scoundrel and for losing his kingdom to his own son.
When Jesus spoke of someone striking you on the right cheek (Matthew 5:39), physical injury wasn't the issue, personal insult was.

B. Slaps are humiliating. To be publicly pelted and insulted by this man was an intense humiliation for the king of Israel. It's difficult to turn the other cheek, not because the slap hurts our face, but because the slap hurts our *pride.*

III. REACTION TO A SLAPPER (v. 9)

A. Abishai wanted to go over to the hill from whence Shimei was chucking rocks, dirt, and insults, so that he could "cut off his head." Abishai was a no-nonsense soldier, one of the infamous, bloodthirsty sons of Zeruiah.

B. Abishai represents the conventional reaction to "slappers," which is retaliation. Our knee-jerk reaction when someone "slaps" us by insult or humiliation is to slap them right back, to put them in their place. There is plenty of applause from the world for those who exact an eye for an eye and a tooth for a tooth.

IV. NOBILITY OF THE SLAPPED (vv. 10-13)

A. The only one that David puts in his place is Abishai. David refuses to allow retaliation and once again entrusts himself to God saying, "It may be that the Lord will see my distress and repay me with good for the cursing I am receiving today" (v. 12).

B. David shows himself to be a man ahead of his time in spiritual maturity. Centuries later Jesus taught, "Blessed are you when people insult you, persecute you and falsely say all kinds of evil against you because of me. Rejoice and be glad, because great is your reward in heaven" (Matthew 5:11, 12). Both the king of Israel and the King of kings knew how to turn the other cheek and were rewarded by God as a result.

V. COMEUPPANCE FOR THE SLAP (19:18-23)

A. When the crises was over for David and he returned to the throne, Shimei got his comeuppance. He prostrated himself before David, begging for mercy. Over Abishai's objections, who still wanted to chop off his head, David pardoned Shimei. However, Shimei later met with a violent death (1 Kings 2:36-46).

B. When we leave vengeance with God where it belongs, those who have persecuted us will get what they deserve. "God . . . will pay back trouble to those who trouble you" (2 Thessalonians 1:6).

ILLUSTRATION

Glutton for punishment. In his first year of college, Bill Jones had not made up his mind as to his future career. He did, however, join the college boxing team. He had a rather good record and was never knocked out during the entire time he participated. At the end of the first college year, Bill's boxing coach took him aside. "Jones," he said, "you have a remarkable constitution. I've seen you take blow after blow and still hang in there. No matter how hard you get punched, you keep coming back. You either have the hardest head I've ever seen or you enjoy getting slapped around!" It was at that point that Bill Jones knew that he was ideally suited to become a preacher!

Keys to Motivation
2 Samuel 18:1—19:8

David was a master of motivation throughout his life. His struggle with Absalom illustrates four important keys to motivation.

I. COMPETENCE (18:1, 2)

A. David demonstrated his competence by mustering his men for battle, organizing them into companies of hundreds and thousands, and sending them out under the tried and true leadership of Joab, Abishai, and Ittai the Gittite.

B. In order to motivate followers, there must be a high level of competence in the leader. Everyone wants to be a part of that which is *well* led, whether it be a military unit, a Little League baseball team, a church choir, or a multi-million-dollar business. Competence leads to high morale.

II. EXAMPLE (18:2)

A. David told his troops, "I myself will surely march out with you." He was a commander who led by example. The exploits of David's "mighty men" included the slaying of giants and killing of lions (2 Samuel 23). In these inspiring efforts, the mighty men were only following in the footsteps of their leader, David.

B. Leading by example is a key to motivation. Jesus expressed scorn for the "leaders" of Israel who were all talk and no action. "You must obey them and do everything they tell you. But do not do what they do, for they do not practice what they preach" (Matthew 23:3).

III. ENCOURAGEMENT (18:3, 4)

A. The army of Israel insisted that David stay behind because he was too valuable to lose. They asked that he give them *support* from the city. "The king stood beside the gate while all the men marched out" (v. 4). Picture David offering words of encouragement to these soldiers as they march out to battle: "You can do it. I believe in you. You're going to win!"

B. Encouragement is a key to motivation. Most people are starving for a word of encouragement. The leader who will express confidence and support to his followers will inspire them to exploits far beyond those of people who are browbeaten, intimidated, or bullied.

IV. PRAISE (18:5–19:8)

A. David's *failure* to praise his men's victory demonstrates the importance of praise as a key to motivation. David was so consumed with his son Absalom's death that he hurt the feelings of the men who had fought so valiantly for him. "For the whole army the victory that day was turned into mourning" (19:2). If Joab had not talked some sense into David so that he praised his men, his entire army would have deserted overnight.

B. Praise is a key to motivation. People are not machines to be taken for granted. People are human beings who want to know that their efforts are appreciated and their work is approved. God motivates his children to live for him with a promise of praise: "Well done, good and faithful servant!" (Matthew 25:21).

ILLUSTRATIONS

Praise motivates in marriage. Norman Vincent Peale: "Praising a woman before marriage is a matter of inclination. But praising one after you marry her is a matter of necessity . . . and personal safety. If you wish to fare sumptuously every day, never knock your wife's housekeeping or make invidious comparisons between it and your mother's. But, on the contrary, be forever praising her domesticity and openly congratulate yourself upon having married the only woman who combines the attractions of Venus, Minerva, and Mary Ann. Even when the steak is leather and the bread a cinder, don't complain. Merely remark that the meal isn't up to her usual high standard of perfection and she will make a burnt offering of herself on the kitchen stove to live up to your ideal of her."

Motivation. A successful chicken farmer increased egg production significantly by posting a sign in the henhouse: "An egg a day keeps Colonel Sanders away."

Passing the Baton

1 Kings 1, 2

David took the necessary steps to place Solomon on his throne as successor. In so doing he models the process for passing the baton of leadership in the church. Let us examine this four-step process together.

I. SEE THE NEED (1:1-27).

A. David was getting "old and well advanced in years" (v. 1). As he weakened, his son Adonijah began to position himself as the new king. The political climate had become confusing and dangerous. Both Bathsheba and Nathan the prophet helped David to see the need to select a new and strong leader: "the eyes of all Israel are on you, to learn from you who will sit on the throne" (v. 20).

B. Leadership in the church must always be aware of the need to reproduce itself. "And the things you have heard me say in the presence of many witnesses entrust to reliable men who will also be qualified to teach others" (2 Timothy 2:2). Without new leadership there is confusion and the danger of division.

II. CHOOSE THE MAN (1:28-31).

A. David did not leave the identity of his successor to chance. "Solomon your son shall be king after me, and he will sit on my throne in my place" (v. 30). David had made a promise to the Lord and to Bathsheba, that of all David's children, Solomon would be the successor.

B. The choosing of servant-leaders for the church is a very important matter in Scripture. "Choose seven men from among you who are known to be full of the Spirit and wisdom" (Acts 6:3). Jesus, Paul, Barnabas, and others modeled the practice of choosing young apprentices into whom they could pour their lives and mentor for future leadership.

III. PRESCRIBE THE CEREMONY (1:32-40).

A. David prescribed the proper ceremony by which Solomon was to be publicly set apart as king. The elements of the ceremony included Solomon's riding on David's mule, his anointing with oil by prophet and priest, the sounding of the trumpet and the shout "Long live King Solomon!" The noise of rejoicing that followed was so great "the ground shook with the sound" (v. 40).

B. The setting apart of believers to positions of important service in God's kingdom has always been accompanied by solemn and earnest ceremony (Acts 6:6; 13:3). This ceremony often includes fasting, prayer, and the laying on of hands. We should not underestimate the importance of ceremony and what it communicates to its object and its witnesses.

IV. GIVE THE CHARGE (2:1-9).

A. David gave an inspiring charge to Solomon. He charged him to be strong and manly. He told him that if he was obedient to God then he would enjoy the Lord's blessing. He asked Solomon to remember old friends with kindness and to beware of old enemies who had caused David trouble.

B. Those to whom we pass the baton of church leadership should receive it with inspiring words of challenge ringing in their ears. Joe Taylor said, "Words have the power to make dance the dullest beanbag of a heart." A charge that communicates passion for God and the things of God will fall on fertile ground and will not soon be forgotten.

CONCLUSION

One of our jobs in leadership is to work ourselves *out* of a job. Pass the baton.

ILLUSTRATIONS

Leadership. Perhaps General Electric CEO Jack Welch explained it best when he said, "The world of the 90's and beyond will not belong to managers or those who make the numbers dance, or those who are conversant with all the business and jargon we use to sound smart. The world will belong to passionate, driven leaders—people who not only have an enormous amount of energy but who can energize those whom they lead."

(Same goes for the church!)

Planning. An old Chinese proverb advises, "If you are planning for one year, grow rice. If you are planning for 20 years, grow trees. If you are planning for centuries, grow men."

Write Your Own Eulogy
2 Samuel 23:1-7

In David's last words, he summarizes his life. This autobiographical summary reads like a eulogy. We should determine to be known for these same five things for which David was known.

I. ONE WHO SANG GOD'S PRAISE (v. 1)
A. David refers to himself with the beautiful title, "Israel's singer of songs." Here he praises God for exalting and anointing him. Of course the Psalms are full of David's songs of thanksgiving and praise to the Lord.

B. At our funerals, may people say of us that in life we sang God's praise. One need not have an exceptional voice to sing God's praise, only a grateful and appreciative heart. As the old hymn says, "Let those refuse to sing who never knew our God!"

II. ONE WHO SPOKE GOD'S WORD (v. 2)
A. Inspired by the Holy Spirit, David actually spoke the Word of God. "The Spirit of the Lord spoke through me; his word was on my tongue."

B. While we are not inspired in that sense today, nevertheless we will want to be known as those who spoke God's Word. Let us speak His Word for comfort, encouragement, teaching, rebuking, correcting, and training in righteousness!

III. ONE WHO BLESSED GOD'S PEOPLE (vv. 3, 4)
A. David blessed God's people through his leadership. Because he ruled in righteousness and the fear of the Lord, he was "like the light of morning at sunrise" (v. 4).

B. We will want to be known as those who blessed God's people. When we use the gift that God gave us to serve the Lord, we'll be a blessing to his church. "Each one should use whatever gift he has received to serve others" (1 Peter 4:10).

IV. ONE WHO ENTERED GOD'S COVENANT (v. 5)

A. David looks back on his life, rejoicing in his covenant with God: "Has he not made with me an everlasting covenant?" As a result of the covenant, David looks forward to salvation and the granting of his every desire.

B. At the end of our lives may others look back on us as those who have entered into a covenant with God. "The covenant of which he [Jesus] is mediator is superior to the old one, and it is founded on better promises" (Hebrews 8:6). Our covenant is founded on the blood of Christ (Matthew 26:28).

V. ONE WHO FOUGHT GOD'S ENEMIES (v. 6)

A. David finishes his eulogy by alluding to the destiny of the enemies of God. They are cast aside like thorns, gathered up with an iron tool, and burned up in the fire. David will always be known as a fierce fighter who was victorious over the enemies of the living God.

B. We should be known as those who gave no quarter to God's enemies—the rulers, authorities, powers of darkness, and spiritual forces of evil. (See Ephesians 6:12.) Like David of old, let us storm the enemies' gates with "weapons of righteousness in the right hand and in the left" (2 Corinthians 6:7).

CONCLUSION

Let us write our own eulogy today and live it out the rest of our lives.

ILLUSTRATION

Setting the right priorities. The lecturer stood in front of his class and said, "Time for a quiz." He pulled out a one-gallon, wide-mouthed mason jar and set it on a table in front of him. Then he produced about a dozen fist-sized rocks and carefully placed them, one at a time, into the jar. When the jar was filled to the top and no more rocks would fit inside, he asked, "Is this jar full?" Everyone in the class said, "Yes."

Then he said, "Really?" He reached under the table and pulled out a bucket of gravel. Then he dumped some gravel in and shook the jar, causing pieces of gravel to work themselves down into the spaces between the big rocks. Then he asked the group once more, "Is the jar full?"

By this time the class was onto him. "Probably not," one of them answered. "Good!" he replied. He dumped sand in, which filled all the spaces between the rocks and the gravel. Then he poured water in that filled it even more.

"What's the point?" he asked. Answering his own question, he continued, "If you don't put the big rocks in first, you'll never get them in at all!"

What are the big rocks in *your* life?